ANNIE SOUTHERN PhD

CAREERING TEENS
Guiding Teenagers' Career Development

This book is dedicated to Ella, Asher and Neve who assisted its development during their teenage years.

Cover and book design Anthony Terry
© Annie Southern, 2014

No part of this publication may be reproduced, stored in a retrieval system or transmitted in any form or by any means, electronic, mechanical, photocopying, recording, scanning or otherwise without the permission of the author.

This material is general in nature. It is made available on the understanding that the author is not thereby engaged in rendering professional advice. Before relying on the material in any important matter, users should carefully evaluate its relevance for their purposes and should always obtain professional advice relevant to their particular circumstances. The material incorporates and summarises views of third parties. Such material is assembled in good faith, but does not necessarily reflect the considered views of the author or indicate a commitment to a particular course of action.

Find out more at anniesouthern.com

Pictures sourced from Depositphotos.com

Pictures © Galina Peshkova (cover), Lisa F. Young, Jean Petrahn, Michael Flippo, Keith Bell, Tyler Olson, Martin Soerensen, Tatiana Kasyanova, Hongqi Zhang, Denizo, Chris Lamphear, Jochen Schoenfel, Woraphon Banchobdi, Federico Caputo, Ralf Cornesse, Angel Nieto, Viktor Cap, Carlos Caetano, Alexey Sizov, Igor Yaruta, Alexey Stiop, Vasyl Nesterov and Francesco Ridolfi.

ISBN: 978-1-5024213-3-3

contents

5	**INTRODUCTION**
5	Information gathering
6	Key figures
6	Following in your footsteps
7	Future focus
8	Finding a direction
9	Getting real
11	Personal issues
13	The first career decision
14	Guiding your teen
16	Finally ...
17	**ACTIVITIES FOR YOUR TEEN**
19	Career daydreams
21	A picture of me
23	Career family tree
25	Career types
27	Personality types
29	Career anchors
31	Career values
33	Parts of a job
35	Job family tree
37	Leisure & work goals
38	**CONCLUSION**
38	**ABOUT AUTHOR**
39	**REFERENCES**
40	**OTHER PUBLICATIONS**

A key part of parenting or caring for older children is being involved in their career decisions. Parents and other caregivers know more about the realities of the world of work than teenagers and can be a useful guide on their career decision-making journey.

introduction

A key part of parenting or caring for older children is being involved in their career decisions. Parents and other caregivers know more about the realities of the world of work than teenagers and can be a useful guide on their career decision-making journey. It has long been said that teenagers need to know that their parents and caregivers are interested in them even if they find it hard to show that they need such engagement. However, it is also important not to be too enmeshed with your teenager by trying to live your career dreams or correct your career mistakes through them.

This book is intended to help you to develop awareness of your teenager's career identity – their values, personality and level of understanding of the world of work – so that you can get a picture of how best to assist them to make successful career decisions. It will help you to learn about their personal career preferences. Through doing the activities in this book you will get a clearer picture of the types of work they would like to pursue and also identify how much more they need to learn about the world of work.

Information gathering

Ginzberg, Ginsburg, Axelrad and Herma have theorised that, from pre-teenhood to young adulthood, individuals pass from a fantasy stage through to a tentative stage and on to a realistic stage. Children are often exposed to information about various occupations through their schooling via school visits by various professionals and through books and media resources. Adults from time to time ask them what they would like to be when they grow up. Answers to these questions change over time as children move away from giving fantasy answers and develop awareness of their interests and, subsequently, when they are older, awareness of their abilities in relation to their interest areas. At the pre-teen point in the child's life (and even into early teenage years) careers such as being a lawyer or a crime scene investigator might seem glamorous because of their profile in television series when the child has very little knowledge of the real tasks involved in the job. In their teenage years, their ideas about work generally become more progressively realistic.

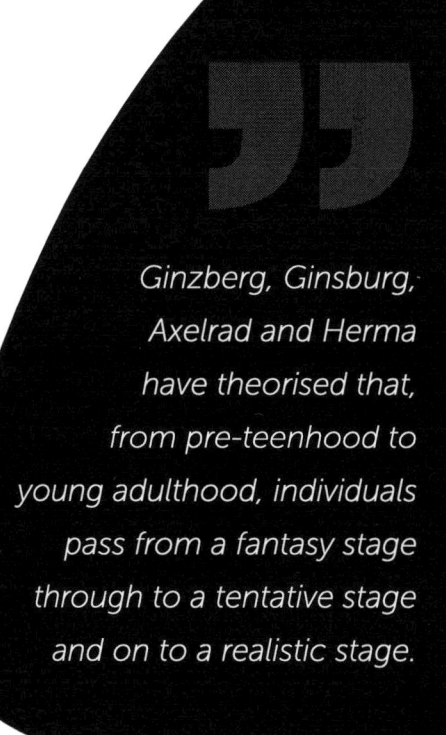

Ginzberg, Ginsburg, Axelrad and Herma have theorised that, from pre-teenhood to young adulthood, individuals pass from a fantasy stage through to a tentative stage and on to a realistic stage.

Key figures

There are often key figures in children's lives who affect how they see their place in the world and how they make sense of it. Usually a key figure will be a parent or caregiver. Often it is a teacher. Sometimes it is a television personality or an authority figure in the community. Children will often imitate key figures and explore their identity through this imitation. Later, as teenagers, they may want to distance themselves from key figures in order to differentiate themselves and find a sense of self. Nevertheless, even if the teenager no longer wishes to imitate them, these key figures may still influence them in many ways (such as the value they give to money or the importance they give to having a good set of work colleagues). Contrary to many parents' and caregivers' beliefs, parents and caregivers (then career advisers, teachers and relatives) have been found to be the main influencers of teenagers' decision-making. Their peers (school mates and friends) are way down the list after these other people, as is the media.

Following in your footsteps

Sometimes a teenager decides early that they want to follow in the footsteps of a parent or caregiver and have the same career. If this decision does not change as they grow older, the teenager is not foreclosing early on their career options. Making sure that the decision is really theirs and not solely a case of imitating a key figure is important. This can be achieved by ensuring that the teenager is very clear about what the job entails, work shadows or interviews people in that profession and has a variety of part time jobs that help them gain realism about the world of work. Having undertaken such measures, if the teenager in their later teenage years still wishes to enter the same occupation as a significant adult in their life, then it can be seen most probably not to be the unsophisticated imitation that a younger child might display.

Future focus

In their early teenage years, teenagers tend to be able to identify what they like to do (interests) but are less clear about what they are good at (abilities). They have come out of the fantasy stage but are still in the tentative stage that Ginzberg, Ginsburg, Axelrad and Herma have identified. As the teenage years progress, they get better at assessing what they are good at, gaining a sense of self-concept and beginning to plan. Their sense of their future becomes more realistic as their teenage years progress.

Often a teenager with no clear career ideas is too focused on living in the present and needs to be given support to become more future-focused. Such teenagers can be engaged too much in leisure and educational activities that do not support planning, goal-setting and consequential thinking. It can be useful to ask yourself: Are they solitary in their leisure pursuits (eg, locked in their bedroom online) or are they members of outgoing recreational groups? Do they have a part time job and have their own money that they have earned or do they still get all of their money from their parents and caregivers? The answer to such questions can indicate if a teenager is engaged in too many behaviours that keep them living in a simple present state (more suited to younger children) without complex future-focused elements to it.

Helping them change their circumstances to make a future-focused orientation a key element in their lives can be helpful. Community involvement is also important to guard against the kind of solipsism (preoccupation with one's wants and desires to the point of egotistical self-absorption) that can lead a teenager to become an adult overly focused on the present moment. Such adults often have little ability to plan in a sophisticated way or delay gratification by saving, goal setting and deferring pleasure in order to pursue vocational credentials and economic security.

A 'planned happenstance' approach can be useful for encouraging future-focused behaviour in your teenager. It is a deliberate way of approaching life where teenagers are encouraged to remain open to chance offers and opportunities by being active in their community (rather than hidden in their bedroom) to catch such opportunities as they come along. An active approach (being available for such opportunities to occur) rather than a passive approach is required to maximise our life's potential. It can be hard work encouraging some teenagers to approach life in this way, but parents and caregivers need to keep trying even if their efforts only get partial results.

> *In their early teenage years, teenagers tend to be able to identify what they like to do (interests) but are less clear about what they are good at (abilities).*

Finding a direction

Despite clearly having values as a child, a teenager will develop their values in a sophisticated and comprehensive way for the first time in their mid-teens. Some of these values can be quite idealistic. This is normal and also admirable even if it can be frustrating to parents and caregivers because it can cause them to come up short in their teenager's estimations. Parents and adults can sometimes be seen to be part of a failing adult population that should have done more in terms of one of their teenager's value areas.

It is important to remember that a teenager is not meant to be fully realistic about what a career entails or how the world works. Their teenage values will reflect this. This is alright as long as they are not also severely misinformed and acting on that misinformation in unhelpful ways. Helping them become informed through their own efforts is the parent's or caregiver's role rather than telling them how little they know or "how it really is in the real world." It can be hard to bite one's tongue and not give teenagers a 'dose of realism' when they are simultaneously both inexperienced and idealistically judgemental. Trying not to be judgmental back can be hard but will prove fruitful.

Teenagers are highly aware of their peers and their place in the world of their peers. They can see that possessions, friendship groups and other affiliations give them prestige. Unlike younger children, they will begin to see that some occupations

Helping them become informed through their own efforts is the parent's or caregiver's role rather than telling them how little they know or "how it really is in the real world."

have more prestige and provide more socio-economic benefits than others. They will come to understand that some jobs take college level education while others do not. They will begin to understand their abilities and assess their interests and values to identify whether further education after leaving school is for them.

Teenagers may come from a family where college education is an unspoken expectation or from a family where working immediately after the school years end is a given. Such expectations will affect their decision-making as to what careers they can consider. The influence of such expectations is not to be underestimated. It can lead a teenager to feel that they have to 'go against' their family or to comply unhappily with their family. Down the track, they may well see that their family's expectations had value, but parents and other adults involved with teenagers need to try to understand the stress that stepping outside the family's approved path may have on a teenager. This stress is genuine even if the teenager is making ill-considered decisions that they will later regret. Teasing out whether the teenager is genuinely oriented to the career path they wish to pursue or is being influenced overly by other key figures, their peers or representations of careers in the media can be helpful.

Some families have stereotyped ideas of occupations in terms of race, gender or social class. In these cases, if a teenager wishes to pursue a job type that the family does not feel is 'fitting', this can cause tension. Alternatively, it can be the teenager who holds stereotypical views about which the family needs to help them become more realistic. Parents and caregivers need to decide carefully when to help their teenager get more information on career issues (to provide them with more options to choose from) and when to let them continue with a career idea that is different from the family's work and study expectations for its members.

Getting real

Young people move from fantasy to tentative to reality stages. The reality stage is made up of exploration, crystallization and specification. Teenager's critical faculties are developing during their teenage years and these faculties become more sophisticated as they move from being teenagers to young adults.

They become more aware of the realities of adult life as these faculties develop. It seems unfair that, with only fledgling abilities for understanding the adult world, teenagers have to make decisions about their future careers. That is, however, what is necessary in a world where vocational roles are no longer limited to following in one's mother's or father's footsteps. Parents and caregivers can help orient teenagers to a career choice by getting them to use information and engage in planning. It is helpful for teenagers to be engaged in some form of employment such as part time baby-sitting, paper rounds, lawn mowing and pet minding. In this way, they will begin to become realistic about what being employed entails in terms of work environments,

The reality stage is made up of exploration, crystallization and specification.

responsibilities, remuneration, undertaking tasks and dealing with employers' expectations. When they reach the legal age to work for a business rather than just doing pet minding and baby-sitting, etc, then part time jobs and short term holiday work can be helpful for teaching teenagers the realities of work.

In this way, they will be more realistic in their career aspirations and learn what they prefer doing (eg, working in an office or outdoors, working alone or being part of a team, working with people, with data or with things). Obviously such part time and holiday jobs are usually relatively unskilled and low paid because they suit school students. So teenagers are only able to do a limited sort of career exploration via such jobs. However, it does help them 'get real' about the world of work and develop good interpersonal communication, time keeping skills, financial responsibility and problem solving abilities. Remember to keep up a conversation with your teenager about what they have learned about the world of work from their holiday and part time work and discuss how their experiences have affected their ideas for jobs in the future.

School careers counsellors can arrange for teenagers to work shadow people in their job or for other types of work experience. They can also be another adult for teenagers to talk to about their career plans other than parents. Careers counsellors are particularly useful for providing educational and occupational information to teenagers through career education programmes at school. They can also explain labour market trends to give teenagers an idea of which jobs are

Remember to keep up a conversation with your teenager about what they have learned about the world of work from their holiday and part time work and discuss how their experiences have affected their ideas for jobs in the future.

currently available and which are less likely to be available to them in the socio-economic environment and geographical location where they live. Careers expos can also be of help to clarify your teenager's ideas and expose them to a wide range of jobs.

Guiding your teenager towards realistic options is important without stamping out the enthusiasm of the teenager who has a clear vocation that they will go to any lengths to achieve. As adults, we can have limited knowledge of some areas of the world of work ourselves without really knowing it. So we should be careful not to clip our teenager's wings career-wise while also providing them with wise counsel and ensuring that the fantasy stage of childhood has fully given way to a sensible exploration phase in adolescence.

Assess your teenager. What context brings out your teenager's best qualities? When do they shine? What makes them happy? What do they do to combat stress? When are they in a flow state that means they do not notice time passing and are fully immersed in some task? What are they skilled at? Can you answer these questions and can your teenager answer them too? If your teenager cannot assess themselves yet, then making good decisions will be hard for them. You can help them by assisting them to get a realistic idea of their abilities when it comes to various types of skills areas and tasks. This will be immensely useful when they look at work options because they will be able to have some idea of whether they could fit into an area of work or not.

Personal issues

If we can send our teenagers out of the nest into the world of work with a sense of self-worth born of feeling competent, purposeful, belonging to a caring social group and clear about their career identity, then we have done a good job. For some parents and caregivers this job will seem reasonably easy. For others, teenagers with personal issues may need help to achieve these things. This may mean dealing with the personal issues first.

Often personal issues lead to a sense of hopelessness and dislocation from family and society. A plan can be helpful to get your teenager through their personal issues and out the other side so that they can then:

- come to see themselves as having competencies
- find a purpose
- identify a group to belong to, and
- gain a sense of what work they would like to do.

A plan can be helpful to get your teenager through their personal issues and out the other side...

> At the end of the teenage years a commitment is usually made to a field of work as their ideas crystalize and they become specific about what job they want to pursue.

A teenager's sense of belonging or alienation depends upon how closely they fit with the normative descriptions of teenagers that they experience via the media, their family/community, their peer group and workplaces. Helping them find environments where who they are is accepted and providing a safe and accepting home life for them can assist them to gain more of a sense of belonging if they seem alienated.

It is often suggested that you try to keep a teenager who has personal issues engaged in the schooling process, if you can, so that they have their schooling as a foundation later when they can look more clearly at career issues. Many people have made career decisions later than the majority because they had personal issues to deal with in their teenage years. They more often than not become competent and contributing members of the workforce as adults.

Literacy and numeracy are key skills and they are one of the things you can improve on if your teenager is lacking direction or not able to make sophisticated career choices because personal issues need to be addressed first. If they need help in the areas of literacy and numeracy, you could hire a tutor or tutor them yourself. Poor numeracy and literacy can have major consequences for a teenager's future career as their choices become much narrower. These two skills — literacy and numeracy — can provide a solid grounding for your teenager in future when they are coping with the constantly changing demands of their roles in the world of work. Literacy and numeracy skills can also prove invaluable in future vocational training since these skills are the foundation to many work-based training situations.

The first career decision

At the end of the teenage years a commitment is usually made to a field of work as their ideas crystalize and they become specific about what job they want to pursue. The first career decision will not be the last. They do not have to get it completely 'right'. Typically, human beings have several jobs over a lifetime, often in different fields. This first teenage career decision — as they enter a college track to a job or enter their first employment situation straight from school — may lead them to a path where they will need to return to study later. An example of this is if they find that progression to higher pay scales or more seniority is precluded in their initial career choice. They may also learn that a job does not entail what they had expected and decide to retrain in a different profession.

Sometimes it is better to guide a teenager who is struggling to make a career decision into a more open-ended work or education decision if they have no clear vocational direction by the time school ends. The economic status of the teenager's family will often come to bear on such undecided teenagers. Sometimes their family's finances mean that they will need to get a good enough job for the time being. Sometimes families can afford for teenagers to stay on in education and go to college to study an open ended subject that does not yet lead them to a career decision but still presents them with options down the track once they graduate.

Guiding your teen

Teenagers are human beings in major transition and they need care and guidance, whether overtly offered and accepted or covertly provided. A few people have always known what they wanted to do for a job and stick to this all their lives, but some people never really have a clear idea. The majority of people, however, work out a direction to take in life in terms of work and refine and adjust this as their life progresses.

At the end of the day, it is really useful to position yourself in your teenager's life as a sounding board and effective helper and this means not acting as too distant and dogmatic an authority figure but rather making your role as a guide attractive to your teenager. This can involve focusing on actively listening, asking questions, assessing where your teenager is 'at' so that you have a sense of their career identity, and taking an encouraging stance in all of your interactions. It is important to respond appropriately to your teenager, which means talking to them at their level of sophistication about the issue of careers, not shaming them for what they do not know yet and their idealism.

A parent's or caregiver's role is often one of offering teenagers opportunities to get more clarity on the careers they are exploring. Building your teenager's self-esteem when they have doubts or fears is important

> *Teenagers are human beings in major transition and they need care and guidance, whether overtly offered and accepted or covertly provided.*

too. You may have to ignore some outbursts born of frustration. Acting as a referral point for your teenager – organising visits to career expos, work shadowing opportunities and informational interviews, and setting up part time jobs – can be a pivotal role for parents or caregivers. Don't just leave it up to the school career adviser. Making sure that a teenager remains engaged in their school work until legal school-leaving age is important too which can be harder for parents of teenagers than parents of younger children. Attending parent evenings and being active in the school community can help you to keep in touch.

Work with your teenager so that they develop their critical thinking skills. Teenagers are naturally wired to want to be critical thinkers. Teenage critical thinking operates in a world of communication through homework assignments, debates with friends, parents, teachers, caregivers and other significant adults, reading articles, going online and watching films and documentaries. There are always other people involved in the writing, reading, listening and talking that goes on in these endeavours. Therefore interpersonal skills and communications skills are also an important area for parents to work on with teenagers.

You may well notice teenagers making statements about current affairs issues. How eloquent are they? Do they stumble over their words and get frustrated because they do not have the words to express what they are trying to say? Do they find it hard to take a discussion on into new territory and extrapolate from their original idea? Teach your teenager to debate with you and to do the research to back up their statements. Work on something they feel passionately about and get them to argue all sides, to read and write about issues, to communicate thoughts and to practice debating with others. Do this in a fun way that involves some banter. This will train them in critical thinking and it can be a good bonding exercise too between you. It can, however,

Work with your teenager so that they develop their critical thinking skills.

be mentally tiring to engage in these kind of discussions and so teenagers may not want to put the effort in. So do make sure you are encouraging discussion of topics they are keen on even if you are not interested yourself. Try not to give speeches and expound on the topic rather than listening and asking questions of your teenager. They are not younger children soaking up what we say as wise older folk anymore. They are teenagers and they want to be doing the thinking and talking if we provide a conducive environment in which they can do this.

Finally ...

So, remember, try to be adaptable and flexible when dealing with your teenager around the issue of careers. Try to keep an open mind. Their career identity may be very different from yours in terms of the job environment they want to work in (office, building site, school, outdoors, etc) and the engagement level they want with others (team work, working alone, working with data or things rather than people, etc). Let them be a different person from you with a different career identity but also protect them from ill-considered choices they may regret later without stifling a genuine vocation. You want a happy adult child in later life. You can do your best to make sure that your teenager is informed and realistic when they choose a career without squashing their enthusiasm and natural teenage idealism. As has been said, teenagers often do not have very detailed knowledge of what they can expect from different job types. It is important to help them 'get real' about these things so that they do not make choices, through lack of information, that they later regret.

Keep an eye on the socio-economic climate and the job market so that you are informed on present trends and not giving your teenager advice based on your school-leaving experience several decades ago. The current socio-economic climate means that companies want leaner staffing structures. This means fewer levels of hierarchy with a lot of middle management jobs disappearing and less vertical promotion these days. People often are moved sideways so horizontal career development opportunities arise. This means that your teenager will most likely work in an environment of ongoing training and retraining and not have as linear a career path as people in the past unless they work in a specific profession such as law or medicine. So their first career choice is just a step along the path of their life-career. Since there are not linear careers so much these days and staying with one company for decades is not the norm anymore, you may find that your child changes career as an adult on average six times in their lifetime. So, even if you do not like their first career choice, they probably will not be doing it in ten years' time unlike people a couple of generations ago.

activities for your teen

This book's activities can help you to work out your teenager's career identity – their values, personality and level of understanding about the world of work. This can help you understand more about how the world of work is viewed from their teenage perspective. While you will get more sophisticated answers from an older teen, it can nevertheless be harder to get them to engage in the activities when they are older. If they need an incentive, try to encourage them to undertake this career identity exploration with you by offering them a movie or a meal or something else they like after doing this work with you.

Don't spend hours doing activity after activity. Break it up into manageable chunks of time so that your teenager remains engaged and happy to be part of the process. Listen to them and let them talk more than you. Make this process as unlike homework as you can in terms of setting, incentives and your demeanour towards them.

You may do an activity in this book and think your teenager's answers show that they need assistance to become more realistic and less fantasy-based in their thinking. You may think that they need to be more future-focused or more informed about the world of work. If so, come back to this 'Introduction' for ideas on how to help your teenager.

The activities in this book are activities you can do several times with your teenager over their teenage years. You do not only have to do them once if you think they will be useful to revisit as your teenager matures.

And remember, you know your teenager best. You are your teenager's best resource. This book is here to help channel your wisdom, not to replace it. Have fun!

Keep an eye on the socio-economic climate and the job market so that you are informed on present trends.

career daydreams

CAREERING TEENS
Guiding Teenagers' Career Development

activity 1

This activity is a good ice breaker.

Ask your teenager to remember when they were a young child and what they wanted to be when they grew up. Get them to write a list of what they wanted to be while you write a list of what you wanted to be when you grew up.

- Share what you have both written.

- Ask them if any of their career ideas as a young child are still of interest to them today.

- Ask what their current ideas are about jobs they would like to do?

- Don't joke about their childhood career fantasies no matter how far-fetched they were. Career daydreaming is important at all times of one's life. Teenagers can be especially sensitive to feeling mocked. Remember that these are their 'child's eye view' ideas of work from when they were younger. Also, do not give a value judgement on their ideas for careers as teenagers today. No matter how unlikely or far-fetched an idea is, it usually provides evidence of a disposition towards something or a core value that an individual holds. If it seems far-fetched then that might be an indicator that you need to work with your teenager on getting more realistic in their thinking about jobs. What childhood career daydreams can provide is a discussion point for what that dream might translate into in a more realistic view of the world.

Is this is an area you need to work on with your teenager to help them become more realistic and have fewer fantasy elements in their current career ideas?

a picture of me

Get a large piece of paper and some pens.

Ask your teenager to draw pictures of themselves (stick figures are fine) in 5 years' time, 10 years' time and 20 years' time. Tell them there are no rules on how to draw the pictures.

- Ask them to explain their pictures to you.

- How well could they see into the future?

- Did they include possessions or other people or buildings and a landscape in their pictures? If not, ask them to draw some in.

- If your teenager did not include objects or other people or a landscape in their pictures and there was just a stick figure or just very stereotypical elements (eg, house, children, car), they may be someone who thinks less tangibly about the scenarios they will find themselves in as an adult. Also, they may not be very future-focused.

- Alternatively, if the people, landscapes, and possessions in the picture mirror a parent's or caregiver's world, this may denote imitation of a key figure. Then again, the people, landscapes, and possessions in the picture may be outlandish and fanciful denoting a fantasy view of adult life that needs to be upgraded to a more realistic view.

- Your teenager may not have a good idea of adult life. That's okay. It will come in time. This activity can give you some insight into how clearly your teenager has an idea of the future for themselves, how mature they are (ie, more realistic and less fantasy-based) and what their aims are or whether they even really have any aims yet. It can give you an idea of the work you need to do with your teenager to get them to be more realistic and also to be future-focused rather than living in the present.

Is this an area you need to work on with your teenager to help them become more future-focused, more realistic or develop their own career identity separate from a key figure?

CAREERING TEENS
Guiding Teenagers' Career Development

activity 2

career family tree

CAREERING TEENS
Guiding Teenagers' Career Development

activity 3

Get some pens and a large piece of paper.

It is useful to get an idea of what messages your teenager has received socially from their family background or the adult influences in their life and the way that these have influenced their beliefs about work and careers. In this activity you will ask your teenager to draw a family tree of all of the jobs their family members have had. If they do not have any family of origin, get them to draw a chart of the jobs of important adults, such as caregivers and family friends, in their lives.

- Ask your teenager to draw a family tree of their family members who are older than them (or a chart of important adults in their lives) and under their names put their main jobs during their lives. You may need to help them research this over a period of days.

- Ask your teenager what kind of messages have been handed down from their family (or important adults in their lives) in terms of work and careers?

- Ask your teenager to write these messages down underneath the names and jobs they have written already.

- Ask your teenager who on the career family tree influences their career decision making the most and in what ways.

- Ask your teenager if there are key figures not on the career family tree that they are influenced by in terms of their decision-making?

Is this is an area you need to work on with your teenager? If they have made a decision to follow a similar path to a key figure, is your teenager engaged merely in imitation or are they making an informed choice? Do you need to work on helping them to move from imitation to an informed position on the influence of adults who are key figures in their life?

Alternatively, the influence of a key figure they dislike might be stopping them from following a similar career that they are, in fact, suited to doing. Does your teenager have some negative or unrealistic views about work that they need to change due to disliking a key figure?

career types

activity 4

CAREERING TEENS
Guiding Teenagers' Career Development

This is a longer activity. So you may wish to break it into two sessions.

Ask your teenager to write a description of what the word 'career' means and then read it to you. Then compare it with the description below. Read the description below out to your teenager or get them to read it to you.

WHAT 'CAREER' MEANS

The term 'career' incorporates work as it intersects with our life roles and social-economic environment. It covers more than just 'jobs'. Your career is your 'self' expressed vocationally and publicly. Here are some ways in which career is seen by different kinds of people:

- a journey
- networking with others
- a cycle
- roles
- an economic resource
- a life story.

▷ Work-life is seen as one of the ways to express our public persona. Home-life is a place where we are more likely to express our private persona. A shy person has a less robust public persona and may seek out jobs that are not social but are more solitary, fitting more with their private persona. Some people have a less confident private self and enjoy the opportunity to express their public self through their workplace and employment.

▷ Different career types have been identified by a variety of theorists over time as suiting different psychological temperaments.

LINEAR

A linear career type explains the conventional notion of upward progression through an organisation from, for example, intern to colleague to supervisor to manager to executive. This type of career is steadily disappearing in a volatile economic environment and as hierarchies in organisations begin to flatten. A career might plateau at a certain point on the linear progression and not move on for a variety of reasons. Professions that can still have a linear track include the military, medicine, education and law.

STEADY STATE

A steady state career type explains the kind of career where development is only undertaken in order to keep one's skills up-to-date, thereby securing ongoing employment. Organisational advancement is less important than enjoyment of one's work. There are a wide variety of such jobs.

SPIRAL

A spiral career type explains a situation where a career in a particular field generalises outwards from a definite role into other roles while remaining in the original field of work. Many careers follow this model as people develop their skills and interests in their chosen field and move around among the various roles available. There is some increase in salary usually with this type of work as time goes on, but not always. Sometimes, people down-size later in life by staying in the same field but taking a less high paying role than they once had.

career types cont.

PORTFOLIO

A portfolio career type is often attributed to consultancy work. Work is project-based and often over-lapping. Self-employed people usually undertake this work. Sometimes people cease to be an employee later in life and become self-employed and adopt this career type.

PATCHWORK

A patchwork career type explains a career based, economically, on the need to adapt to economic variables and survive financially or psychologically. No discernible patterning is identifiable in hindsight.

- Ask your teenager about people they looked at in Activity 3. What types of career do they think those people have had – linear, steady state, spiral, portfolio or patchwork? They may have had more than one type.

- Ask your teenager what career type they would prefer to have.

- Ask your teenager what kinds of career types – linear, steady state, spiral, portfolio, patchwork – are most available in their geographical location and the current job market.

- Ask your teenager to go through the newspaper or an online job service and name the kinds of career types (linear, steady state, spiral, portfolio, patchwork) from a page of different jobs.

- Getting your teenager to think about careers as outlined in the description 'What Career Means' helps them to 'get real' about career options since it makes them think about what type of career a job fits with best.

Is this is an area you need to work on with your teenager? How easily did your teenager understand the description? If they did not find it easy to understand and then answer the questions after it, have ongoing discussions with them where you both look at jobs in 'situations vacant' listings and discuss the career types the jobs belong to. Often a job can belong to more than one career type. You may also wish to do more work with them (through online research or reading relevant magazine and newspaper articles) so that they understand the labour market today.

personality types

CAREERING TEENS
Guiding Teenagers' Career Development

activity 5

PART ONE

- Ask your teenager which of the following they would prefer to work with? Get them to rank them in order of preference 1, 2, and 3:
  - data – theorising, reporting, researching, writing, calculating
  - people – helping, serving, supporting, healing, leading, selling to
  - tangible things – animals, objects, machines, food, art, clothes

- Ask them to write a list of what types of jobs would allow them to work with their preference.

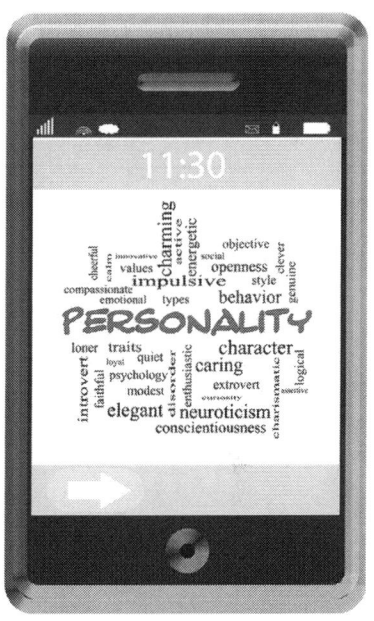

PART TWO

Next, read out 'Holland's Personality Types' to your teenager or get them to read it to you.

HOLLAND'S PERSONALITY TYPES

A career theorist called John Holland believed that both people and work environments can be assessed as:

- Realistic
- Investigative
- Artistic
- Social
- Enterprising
- Conventional.

Holland felt that an individual will be a mix of three of the types as will a job environment, with a weighting for one type more than the others.

Realistic (R) are people who like nature, or athletics, or tools and machinery.

Social (S) are people who are drawn to helping, teaching, or serving others.

Investigative (I) are people who are very curious, like to investigate or analyse things.

Enterprising (E) are people who like to start up projects or organizations, and/or influence or persuade people.

Artistic (A) are people who are very artistic, imaginative, and innovative.

Conventional (C) are people who like detailed work, and like to complete tasks or projects.

personality types cont.

Holland described the relationship between personality and occupation with a hexagonal model where closely related types were adjacent and types expected to be unrelated were opposite. Many job allocation tools, both paper-based and computer-based, have Holland's underlying schema as their basis.

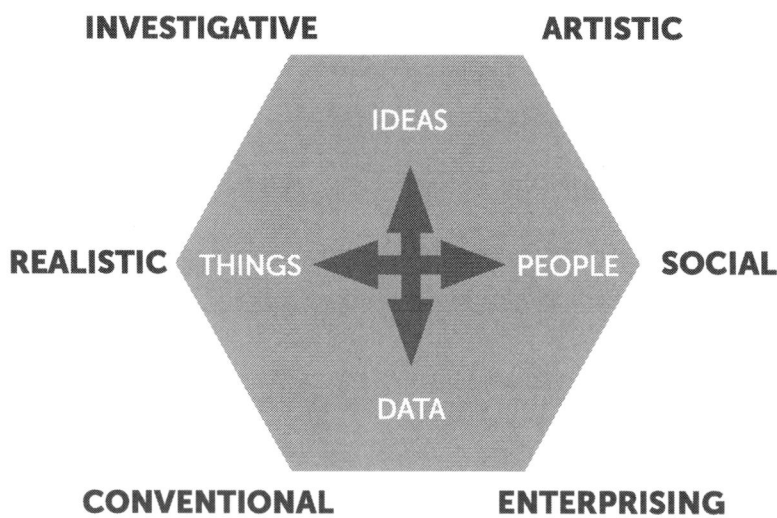

- Ask your teenager which three of these Holland personality types (Realistic, Investigative, Artistic, Social, Enterprising and Conventional) they think they are most like.

- Ask them which they think is their main Holland personality type.

- Ask your teenager to name three jobs that would suit their main Holland personality type. How do these jobs compare to the jobs they thought of in Part One?

- Ask your teenager which of these Holland personality types (Realistic, Investigative, Artistic, Social, Enterprising and Conventional) they think the people on their family tree are in Activity 3.

Could your teenager identify which Holland personality type(s) they are and see what type of jobs would suit their personality type best? Is this is an area you need to work on with your teenager to help them grasp the idea of different types of personalities fitting with different types of jobs? If they are unclear, you could look through job vacancy listings and ask them to say which of Holland's personality types goes best with the different jobs and whether those jobs work with data, people or tangible things.

career anchors

activity 6

CAREERING TEENS
Guiding Teenagers' Career Development

Read out the following to your teenager or get them to read it to you.

SCHEIN'S CAREER ANCHORS

A career theorist called Edgar Schein feels that an individual's core values, motivations, and physical and psychological needs serve to provide a springboard from which career decisions are made. He sees career anchors as underpinning our career thoughts and behaviour and lists them as:

- *Technical/functional competence* (enjoying being good at one's work).

- *General managerial competence* (pursuit of success and using problem-solving skills as an executive leading others).

- *Autonomy/independence* (a need to work to one's own agenda, usually alone).

- *Security/stability* (a need for stable income without major psychological upheavals and economic risks).

- *Entrepreneurial creativity* (a need to be inventive, own one's ideas and products and achieve wealth as a sign of success, while employing others to increase one's productivity and economic base).

- *Service* (dedication to a cause with a view to helping others and less importance on power, prestige and wealth).

- *Pure challenge* (the need for constant stimulation; high level problem-solving and risk taking for psychological stimulation as much as economic gain).

- *Lifestyle* (the need for integration of one's entire way of living, where the lines between work and other aspects of life become blurred).

- Ask your teenager which of these career anchors fits them best (there may be more than one).

- Ask them to choose their main career anchor if they chose more than one.

- Ask your teenager which of the three jobs that they thought matched their personality in Activity 5 matches their main career anchor the most here in Activity 6.

Is there a good fit between the career anchor they chose and the jobs they thought of in Activity 5? If not, then they may not have a realistic view of the jobs or they may still be struggling to have a clear idea of their values and their self-concept. That is okay. These thing develop over time, but you can help them by getting them to explore the world of work through work shadowing, informational interviewing, or a short term holiday job or part time job in order to help them get more information on jobs. Then try Activities 5 and 6 again with them.

career values

CAREERING TEENS
Guiding Teenagers' Career Development

activity 7

In this exercise you get to explore what your teenager wants from work. This is what values are in career development. Values are not just ethical concerns. Values define what kind of person your teenager is and how that can be expressed best in the world of work so that they are happy and successful.

LIST ONE

Good workplace fit for the employee can often be due to flow experiences on the job. The psychologist Mihaly Csikszentmihalyi interviewed people who described their optimum experiences using the metaphor of being carried along on a current – being totally immersed in what they were doing and being successful in the endeavour. From this the term 'flow' was developed.

- Ask your teenager to write down lists of activities they would do for free, activities they would pay to do or nag parents or caregivers to let them do and activities where they lose track of time.

- Ask them if any of these activities could be turned into a job or sound like activities that could be a part of jobs.

You may not get a serious answer to this question, in which case do not worry. Sometimes teenagers just give fantasy answers. But, sometimes, it can identify activities that a teenager loves doing that can be geared towards the world of work.

LIST TWO

Show your teenager this list of things that can be gained from a career:

1) money, vacations, a house, a good car
2) security
3) freedom and options to choose for myself
4) status, praise and fame
5) purpose, meaning, self-expression
6) power and influence
7) travel, new horizons, other cultures
8) like-minded people, friendship, a social life, belonging

- Ask your teenager what other things not on the list above they are looking for from work.

- Ask your teenager to rank the things on the list that can be gained from a career from most important to them to least important to them.

- Ask your teenager what types of jobs would allow them to work with their top three ranked items in List Two. How do these jobs compare to the jobs they thought of in Activities 5 and 6?

What have you learned about your teenager's career values from this activity? If they are a younger teenager, this activity will yield less certain answers. Is your teenager still fantasising when they answer these questions or are they more realistic in the answers they gave? Often it is the conversation around their answers that shows you where they are 'at' in terms of career maturity and whether they need help to develop more mature values beyond the fantasy level. All teenagers should have fewer fantasy elements to their answers and more to say about their values as they get older. Do your teenager's answers show that they can express themselves maturely in a way that fits with them being a teenager beginning to prepare for the world of work? If not, do they need to be given opportunities such as work shadowing, informational interviewing and part time jobs to learn more about the world of work so that it becomes more real to them? Also, do they need help becoming more future-focused?

parts of a job

CAREERING TEENS
Guiding Teenagers' Career Development

activity 8

Many teenagers have unrealistic views about work and careers. For example, they may think that the job of a crime scene investigator seems glamorous because they see this job type portrayed as glamorous on television shows. In reality, it is quite different and involves a lot of science and report writing. How much clarity does your teenager have about what jobs entail?

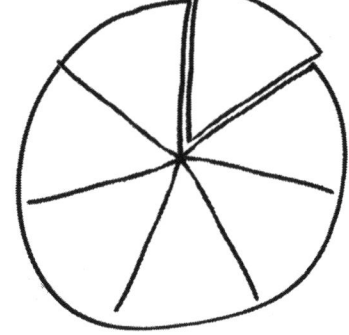

Get a large piece of paper and some pens.

JOB ONE

Ask your teenager to draw a pie with seven pieces to it like the one on this page.

- Ask them to choose a job they wanted to do when they were a child (one of the jobs from Activity 1).

- Ask them to note down in the segments of the pie seven aspects of the job, putting the most important aspect of the job in the separate piece of the pie.

- Ask them to do some research online if necessary (with your help if they want it) to find out more about this job and to check if their answers were accurate.

JOB TWO

Ask them to choose a job that someone on their family tree in Activity 3 has done and re-do the exercise.

JOB THREE

Ask them to do the activity again for the job of being a lawyer (unless it has already been covered in which case choose another job).

EVALUATION

- Ask your teenager if they are put off or attracted to any of the jobs they have looked at in this activity because of what they involve (for example, the work environment being indoors/outdoors, the tasks involved, the geographical location of jobs, the interactivity with people being minimal or constant).

- Ask your teenager which of the Holland personality types (in Activity 5) the three jobs they have looked at in this activity match the best.

- Ask your teenager which career anchors (in Activity 6) the three jobs they have looked at in this activity match the best.

- Ask your teenager which of the three jobs they have looked at in this activity would most provide them with the things they said were most important to them in Activity 7, List Two.

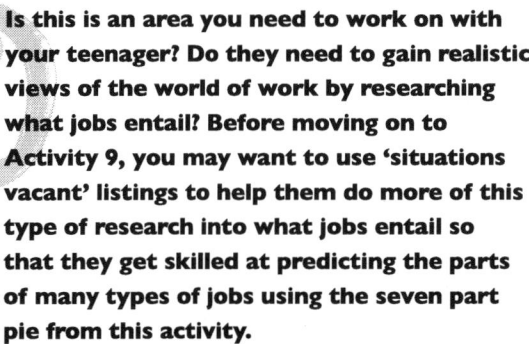

Is this is an area you need to work on with your teenager? Do they need to gain realistic views of the world of work by researching what jobs entail? Before moving on to Activity 9, you may want to use 'situations vacant' listings to help them do more of this type of research into what jobs entail so that they get skilled at predicting the parts of many types of jobs using the seven part pie from this activity.

job family tree
activity 9
CAREERING TEENS
Guiding Teenagers' Career Development

This activity leads on from Activity 8 and gets more 'real' about what jobs involve. Tell your teenager that they can use this activity to research jobs they are interested in so that they know as much as possible what is involved. If they need to do research online to complete the activity that is fine. By using this activity whenever they consider a job, your teenager can find out what a job really entails and whether it fits with their values and personality.

Teenagers will often think about jobs rather than professions, but if they can think about professions it gives them more of an idea of the range of movement career-wise that they could have in the future if they choose to have a portfolio or spiral career or move upwards in a linear career (as discussed in Activity 4).

PART ONE
Get a large piece of paper and some pens. Ask your teenager to draw the following diagram for the profession of being a lawyer (they looked at this in Activity 8 - Job 3).

- Tell them to put the profession (law) at the top and then draw under it the different fields within that profession (eg, criminal law, property law, family law). Then under each field put the kinds of job (eg, lawyer, barrister, legal clerk). Next to each job put the activities (tasks and roles) of that kind of job and next to each activity put the skills required.

- Ask your teenager to look at the activities and skills required for being a lawyer and ask them whether they would want to do those activities or study to learn those skills.

How much congruence (fit, match) is there between the job they chose in 'Part Two' and their main Holland personality type, their career anchors and their career values? If there is not much of a fit, then get them to do more research into their job choice in this activity in case it is an unrealistic choice for them based more on fantasy or the influence of others rather than their own career identity as it is emerging in their teenage years.

PART TWO
On another piece of paper, ask your teenager to draw a diagram for a different profession – one that they are interested in, eg, education, construction, the creative arts, government service, sports, entertainment.

- Ask them to put the particular profession they are interested in at the top and then draw under it the different fields (areas of practice) within that profession. Then under each field put the kinds of jobs possible within the profession. Next to each job put the activities (tasks and roles) of that kind of job and next to each activity put the skills required.

(NB. If it is easier to start by writing down the job, eg, actor, ask them to fill in the fields and the profession above that job afterwards, eg, profession = arts; fields = theatre, film, advertising, educational.)

- Ask your teenager how this job they are interested in fits with their main Holland personality type in Activity 5.

- Ask your teenager how the job fits with the career anchor they felt most suited them in Activity 6.

- Ask your teenager how the job (and the activities and skills it requires) fits with their career values as they expressed them in Activity 7, List Two.

leisure & work goals

activity 10

CAREERING TEENS
Guiding Teenagers' Career Development

This final activity should be a fun activity after some of the hard work of the other activities.

- Ask your teenager to write down three lists of their work and leisure goals for the following: now, in a year's time and in 3 years' time.

- Ask your teenager to find a selection of pictures from magazines that inspire them and reflect what they want out of life now, in a year's time and in 3 years' time in terms of leisure and work.

    (NB. These pictures might take them some time to collect so make this a project and tell them to take their time over it.)

Get a piece of art paper, some scissors and some glue.

- When they have the pictures they want, ask them to cut out the parts of the pictures they like that fit with their goals and create a collage of inspirational images that reflects their goals for the next 3 years, starting with now on the left and moving in time across the page until they reach 3 years' time on the right.

- Ask them to put this picture up somewhere to inspire them and to remind them of their work and leisure goals.

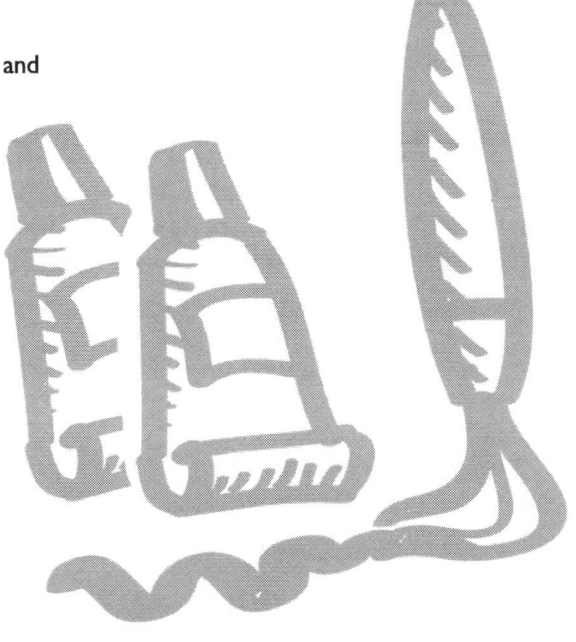

conclusion

While your teenager is still at school it is useful early on to ask them to list their subject choices, the jobs that interest them and the school subjects or training courses that these jobs require (this might require some research on their part). At each subject choice stage in their schooling, ensure that the subjects they are taking at school really fit with the types of jobs/careers that match the values, personality type and career anchors of your teenager as you have been able to ascertain them from doing the activities in this workbook. If you feel there is some lack of fit, guide your teenager into learning experiences and activities that help them to get real about the world of work. Then check with them again that they are taking the right school subjects for their future career options.

Remember to be aware of the level of career maturity of your teenager and keep conversations appropriate for that level. If you feel they are not exhibiting the sort of maturity around career issues that they should have at their age, then work with them to find out more clearly the truth about their career identity in terms of their personality, values and career anchors. Run through the activities in this book with them as often as you need during their teenage years so that you can see how their career maturity is developing. They may well thank you for it down the track.

Annie Southern, PhD

> *At each subject choice stage in their schooling, ensure that the subjects they are taking at school really fit with the types of jobs/careers that match the values, personality type and career anchors of your teenager as you have been able to ascertain them from doing the activities in this workbook.*

about author

Dr Annie Southern was educated at Oxford University and has a PhD in health science from the University of Canterbury. She has undertaken doctoral research in the career development field and has given talks on career development for counsellors, career professionals, parents and the general public as well as writing several career development workbooks for various groups. Her books are available in both print and ebook formats.

Find out more at anniesouthern.com

references

Csikszentmihalyi, M. (1975). *Beyond Boredom and Anxiety: Experiencing flow in work and play.* San Francisco: Jossey-Bass.

Csikszentmihalyi, M. (1990). *Flow: The psychology of optimal experience.* New York: Harper & Row.

Ginzberg, E., Ginsburg, S.W., Axelrad, S., & Herma, J.L. (1951). *Occupational Choice: An approach to a general theory.* New York: Columbia University Press.

Holland, J.L. (1973). *Making Vocational Choices: A theory of careers.* Englewood Cliffs: Prentice-Hall.

Krumboltz, J.D. & Levin, A.S. (2004). *Luck is No Accident: Making the most of happenstance in your life and career.* Atascadero, CA: Impact Publishers.

Parsons, F. (1909). *Choosing a Vocation.* Boston: Houghton Mifflin.

Schein, E.H. (1990 & 1996). *Career Anchors (Discovering your real values).* Hoboken, NJ: Jossey-Bass Pfeiffer.

Schein, E.H. (1996). Career anchors revisited: Implications for career development in the 21st century. *The Academy of Management Executive,* 10(4), (November 1, 1996), pp.80-88.

other publications

Explore Your Career Identity: A Practical Workbook

Paperback and ebook

Explore Your Career Identity: A Women's Workbook

Paperback and ebook

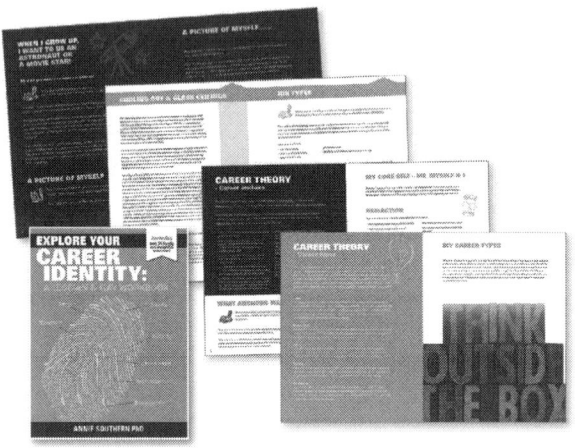

Explore Your Career Identity: A Lesbian & Gay Workbook

Paperback and ebook

Explore Your Career Identity: A Mental Health Workbook

Paperback and ebook